INTERTWINED

DR. MALABIKA MITRA

notionpress
.com

INDIA • SINGAPORE • MALAYSIA

ISBN 979-8-89415-618-7

For my husband Vijay,
for you I live

Contents

Contents

Contents

Thank You

I am very grateful to my parents for their unconditional love, for being my pillar of strength and for always being there for me, without whom I would not have been here today…

My gratitude and thanks to Babita Rajkhowa from *The Assam Tribune*, Nurul Islam Laskar from *The Sentinel* and Indrani Rai Medhi also from *The Assam Tribune* for their love and support; to my teachers of English literature, especially Ranjit Chowdhury, Pradip Acharya, Aditi Chowdhury, Prof. Arthur Lindley and Padma Shri Late Temsula Ao for their invaluable mentoring during my college and varsity days, and last but not the least, my friends Prof. Shakuntala Mahanta, Anju Darshini, Shilpa Menon, Fateha Haque, Rituparna Goswami Pande, Tasrina Iqbal, Karabi Bharali, Suman Sarma (from *The Guwahati Grand Poetry Festival*), Lakshmy Shankar, Garima Sinha, Malini Sangeneni, Divya Varadarajan and Rekha for believing in me.

How can I forget, my daughter Radha for her intelligent, quick and timely responses, whenever, I was in need of them…

And of course, to the team at Notion Press for making this publication possible.

Author's Note

Of You and I
&
Dear Life

Ups and downs are inevitable in life. But the strange thing about them is that they appear to be unending – especially the downs – as time seems to drag on a tad longer when caught-up in this quagmire, whereas, happy times just seem to whizz by. Indeed, the downs can be so abysmal at times, that the ups appear nowhere in sight… a time when one almost succumbs to despair and loses hope. But when you hit the rock bottom, you reach a point where you can go down no further. Henceforth, you only rise.

As my days began to lighten up filled with hope, and I turned a new leaf, I began to dabble with verse. I had not the slightest idea that I could compose verses, staccato at best. I have not yet summoned up the courage to call my scribblings as either poems or verses. They are just mere ramblings to myself which I managed to jot down. But deep within, I had cherished the thought, that one fine day, I would manage to put a few of them together, to make a volume.

By the time I had written the first composition of this work, I was already an established freelancer back home, (being any day, more comfortable with prose, which generally speaking, can be much simpler, much less riddled than poetry) as my articles on various topics from women, to empowerment, to culture, literature and book reviews were published regularly in the supplements of prestigious and widely-circulated newspapers of North-East India like *The Assam Tribune* and *The Sentinel*.

However, I held on to my poems for long, not letting them out of the confines of my laptop. It was much later, that I finally decided to test the water. Thus, a couple of them were published in *The Assam Tribune*, in the coffee-table magazine *Eclectic* and much later online, in the poetry forum of *The Guwahati Grand Poetry Festival*. But such publications were rare. Those few which were printed have been duly acknowledged along with the respective pieces.

The compositions in this collection, were not written in one go; but have spanned for almost two decades. There were moments, when in a burst of creativity, I would put my thoughts down, one after the other, in a matter of days. But there were also phases when I had not written a word in a year. Terrible mood swings and mindless pre-occupations! Now that I come to think of it.

But then, where else lies the germ of a poem if not in mood swings, eccentricity, hope and despair. Yes, melancholy, if not despair! The best of verses, when we look back at our great masters of the past, have often had an underlying tone of melancholy. True, there was light and gloom dispelled, but somewhere, deep down a capacity to look at the uncheerful side of life resided in me. I attribute that to my innate nature, since I fail to explain it otherwise. Some of the poems here are hopeful, fewer has a tone of humour and most has an underlying sadness, despite the sunshine.

My thoughts that found expression in words; my ramblings, as I would prefer to call them have all originated from observations of life around me, arising from specific situations, common-place feelings, emotions and objects; and hence, many of you, dear readers, will be able to relate to. After all, aren't our lives *intertwined*.

Wishful as it might be, I dare to hope that this volume, will make you pause and reflect at life's journey with its many twists and turns. Keeping fingers crossed, I also hope it will not disappoint those who have cared to be a part of my thoughts and reflections, by picking up this book.

I did love to hear from you…

01

Silent Yearnings*

Breakfast is served
Table laid –
Bowl laden with ripe fruits alluring,
Chilled red juice of melons
Tempting and provoking,
Eggs poached to perfection
Ready to dribble
As, I await
A moment with my beloved
To be heard, to be loved, to be held.

You tell me last night
The night before,
And, the night night before
You are tired
Too tired after a long day
To talk to me
Hence, shall we talk tomorrow;
Months, thus, have gone by
Awaiting the morning tomorrow
For the long-yearned moment
When you shall listen to me
Hold me close,
As never to part away.

Yet the morning never came
You never cared enough
To listen to the meanings that made my day,
The story of my heart,
All that my soul
Wanted to scream out
Had so much to say...
Of dreams unrealized,
Now crushed and forgotten lay.

The table thus laid
I waited for you,
It has been so long lest I forget;
Not just to have breakfast with you,
Yearning deep down, for a word from you,
To be in your arms
Encircled in love.
But for you, my dear
Where is the time,
Mustn't you not hurry by.

Yet I like to fool myself,
A hopeless lover,
Indulging in fantasies
Of a lover besotted,
Yearning silently,
For all that love promises
But never can be,
For what the breakfast was,
What it could be…

*   *This poem was selected amongst top 10 in English and top 25
from over all languages for the Indian Writer's Award 2024,
by Indian Film House.*

02

Till the Other Day

It was all over
Or, so I thought
Like the dead Bael* tree that I see from my window
Laden with green fruits
Which unripe shall remain
To wither, wrinkle and die.

Hope and promises were alien,
And how can it not be?
In a life like the dark, dreary corridors of the hospital
Hoping only to survive
Certain that survival alone, shall it be
In a life that fails to be lived!

Celine Dion's songs kept ringing in my ears
Of love, to believe in love
A hundred other like-emotions;
I dismissed them as unreal, as impossible
For they were meaningless to me.

The romantic in me
Had died long ago,
And so it would remain, I was sure –
A broken heart, trapped,
But not old enough to die.

It was so, till the other day
When you walked into my life
Changing life for ever,
When I least expected.
God's gift, a miracle or destiny
I cannot say
Nor do I wish to know
So long, you are by my side
Inspiring me to love, to live
To have faith
And, be US.

*   Bael – wood apple in Bengali and Assamese languages. A fruit also
often offered to Lord Shiva by his devotees.

03

Voices

The soft hum I hear
Is from the AC,
But wait!
No, it comes from elsewhere –
Incoherent, unclear voices of the multitude
Rumbling, growing louder
Like approaching thunder clouds
Waiting to break loose.

Voices of dissent
Of anger, displeasure, disagreement,
Perhaps jealousy too;
Wrapped in confusion
Only breeding more.
Lost, restless, and in *ashanti**
Where happiness remains elusive
The search for it
A distant dream.

We walk hand-in-hand,
Through crowded streets
Narrow lanes;
In evenings
That reminds of Eliot's Prufrock[*1],
You ask me to be patient

Assure, it is but a matter of time
Before the voices fade.

Your confidence is infectious,
Yet I feel scared,
That they may overpower –
Our dreams, happiness and hopes
Whose fragility never endures;
Here uncertainty rules
And future, forever, an enigma.

I know, of cruel fate
Of love's suffering, humiliation and defeat,
But history also whispers,
Tales, of love everlasting,
Till the age of time.

So long as voices are heard,
Our aspirations unfulfilled
A distant future;
Come, my love
You and I will close our ears
And immerse in our moment.
Let those voices humour themselves
We can shut them out
Seeking comfort in ourselves,
Fulfilment, in our love.

*   ashanti – antonym for shanti or a deep sense of peace
*1 Elliot's Prufrock – reference is to the American – British poet and
critic's ground-breaking poem *The Love Song of J. Alfred Prufrock*

04

The Beginning – The Journey

The break of dawn, it was,
Maybe, even moments earlier,
Fresh as any beginning can be
The darkness fading away,
The soft light emerging
Of a promising new day.

Together we passed –
Deserted streets
As street lights dimmed away,
A few stray dogs only, for company,
It was just you and I,
So peaceful, so serene, so pure
As if the whole city
Nay, the whole world
Belonged to us.

We were expectant,
An expectancy like never before,
Thrilling yet comforting.
We went along,
Strong in belief
To face, overcome and succeed.

My mind travelled to the night,
For it was a difficult night
Which brought us together,
Making possible for us
This new day;
The journey ahead
Is long,
This is the start
That you and I shall travel
As one,
From dawn, till the end of night.

Towards our goal we moved,
Through streets, lanes and by-lanes –
Gradually waking up, coming alive;
Lush fields
Others being brought to life,
With flowers and fruits sprinkled
On trees, shrubs and bushes
At some turns,
In corners, and pathways
Some visible, others not.

Ahead is a hill
That we climb,
To seek His blessings
He, who will lead us along.
Stop, we might
To pause, think, rejuvenate and start anew
Leading us on.

Towards His misty abode
Through white wispy clouds.

Ethereal, striking, majestic
Rugged but cultivated
You show me on.
Here we begin
At His feet
A new day; a new life
The beginning – the journey.

05

O Peace!

'What is peace?', they ask,
Children of today
To children of yesterday;
Hoping to find an answer –
But how can we,
A generation lost, ignorant
Spreading and teaching
Only that we know
Hatred, anger and chaos.

Blame us not,
We are not totally to blame;
For this balmy experience
Eluded us too.
A gift from our fathers, forefathers
Generations uncountable and innumerable
That failed to live together
To live as brothers
Sinning against God
Against humanity.

Lessons, no matter how harsh
Left us untaught;
Words of wisdom, unheeded
Prophets and scriptures dismissed,
As swords were drawn

Guns fired and bombs dropped.
A generation lost,
Unsure of itself
Unable to look back
Or, usher a bright tomorrow.

Curfews, bandhs, strikes,
Explosions and encounters
Here a child first learns.
Along with cartoons
He watches too,
People killed here and there
Victims of wrath, of IEDs, of suicide bombers.
Is this heaven, earth or hell, she asks,
Or, is hell a state of mind,
As an angry poet*, once said
Through his rebel hero,
Hundreds of years ago.

Our eternal search have failed
As white grows paler,
Red bouncing with renewed vigour.
Here peace remains a distant cry,
Today, as it always was –
Perhaps, to remain
An eternal quest
Like the Holy Grail;
Doomed to be thwarted
Now, forever and forever.

*   John Milton and his epic poem *Paradise Lost*

Published in *The Assam Tribune*

06

Autumn Fury

September is the cruellest month,
Not April, as a poet-critic had told*,
For autumn is about –
Struggling to survive
In blazing paddy fields, parched bamboo groves,
As clay walls begin to crack;
All around geared to spark
To spread the heat,
Add to our miseries.

Where is the "season of mists"?
"Of mellow fruitfulness"*1, I search,
Of which were promised centuries ago;
Instead, here are hot summer afternoons
The strong rays of the autumnal sun,
And an eternal wait for respite,
Without guarantee, without succour;
Without rain too, yet excruciatingly humid
Turning into a desert, a tropical plain.

Dust, silt and dry earth
Takes over all,
Jelabis*2 sold in grimy street corners,
Women on way to work,
Spreading with equal smoothness

Over her lipstick, her made-up face,
Her cleavage;
Conquering with equal proficiency,
Also Japanese displays
In a living room cabinet.

Suddenly a fire breaks out
Waking you up, in the middle of the night;
To your shock and alarm
Discover, all that is precious, is prized
Turned to heap, to cinders.
The blazing fury continues,
Rapidly, devastatingly, to consume
Homes and businesses, paints and files,
Now made perfectly crisp and dry,
Victims of rainlessness.

A once handsome man,
Now old, tired, and frail
Watches from a distance, helplessly
This fury ablaze;
Unsure, of ever recovering
What he loses.
Sympathizers, curious observers,
Hover close by –
Shrewd insurance officers too,
Are spotted, looking for profit
From another's misery.

'Where is justice?', I ask,
As Mother Goddess Durga
Comes shortly visiting,
On her yearly sojourn.

Reminding us of Her victory
Her conquest over evil.
Yet today, I see Her smile
Forever, an enigmatic smile,
Her eternal wisdom sees
The world unchanged,
Pathetic, cruel, unloving,
Ever poor in feelings and emotions,
Just the way it always was
And, will always be.

These tales She recounts,
In the comfort of Her Himalayan retreat,
Ten days later;
Waiting eagerly to return, in a year's time –
To check our materialistic world,
In another September,
In another autumn fury.

[*]   Reference is to T.S. Eliot's *The Waste Land*
[*1] Remembering John Keats words on autumn from his poem "Ode
      to Autumn"
[*2] Jelabis – an Indian sweet that is crispy, juicy and comes in circles.
      Often found being sold on the Indian roadside.

Published in *The Assam Tribune*.

07

Still Waiting

I was waiting,
Rejoicing
To see you,
Have you with me,
Waiting for you to come,
Instead, you called –
You, were not coming.

Suddenly, the world turned meaningless,
Life bereft of colours,
An emptiness within, I felt
That seemed to swallow me up.
I worked listlessly
For the chores must be completed,
Yet I was not of this world,
Knew not what I did,
Vague, spiritless; becoming only a shadow of me.

It was last month,
When we got to know the other,
But today, it seems long ago
To be away, away from you;
Yearning, not knowing
When my eyes can rest on you.

Sweetest, I blame you not,
For you are not to blame.
It was unforeseen;
But why, did Mother Nature play truant
With our hopes, our feelings,
The lives of many?
You tell me of villages
That now stands destroyed,
Lifeless bodies of children, women and young men,
Wrapped in mud and dirt
Waiting to return to dust.

Their misery is greater
More devastating, more shattering
Than our own,
Surviving from makeshift camps
With no homes, food or clothes to call their own.
You too sounded painfully sad,
When you spoke,
Still we both gave each other hope,
Trying to comfort the other's sorrow
As we hid our own.

You blame yourself
For disappointing me;
But you, my dear,
Never disappoint me.
For you I wait
Till eternity if need be,
While something within says,
That you will be here, and very soon too,

To wake me up one morning
With a sweet kiss,
But until then,
I am, still waiting.

08

Death Comes Calling

You were but a stranger
To me, till the other day,
I heard your whisperings
Knew of your presence;
Your occasional visits to the neigbourhood –
Among acquaintances and strangers,
Sudden, untimely, even expected,
Of your playful side too!
Your love for raising a false alarm,
Fickleness of temperament,
Preference to revise and alter
Decisions at will.

These tales told and retold
By those, familiar to you
For you are unforgettable;
Leaving ever a mark,
An influence, an impression
Even with your slightest touch,
When you come calling
Knocking at our doors.

True, you are all these, nothing less,
The experience of a life-time;
With a hint of glamour too,
As poor Emily's* lover

And William S.'s[*1] obsession;
Rubbing shoulders with the rich and famous,
Forever remaining
A popular figure of public importance too,
The talk of town
Hotly discussed, debated and powerful
Over the nameless multitude.

These privileges you enjoy
But you are judicious true,
Albeit, strangely though –
For you know no discrimination
Visiting with equal regularity the less fortunate too,
Never failing to call on all of us,
Mocking us for our un-preparedness,
As we, are never ready to receive you.
Some wait for you to come
While others you choose, at your own sweet will,
To take by surprise;
Yet you come calling
And unfailingly too.

But today, I find you
Injudicious, unjust,
Capable of causing grief, creating emptiness;
Your sudden short visit
Leaving a lot unanswered,
Grief untold, my dear ones lost.

Today I strip you off your glamour,
Instead, to be feared, held in awry,
Shunned and carefully avoided –
When in a mad frenzy

You see no rhyme or reason,
But simply carry on.
Yet I know –
Of your unfailing visit,
Surely you will come again
To leave behind an injury
That you alone
Can wipe away.

*   Emily Dickinson, American poet; her poems bring out her fascination with death. In some, death is depicted as a lover too.

*1   William Shakespeare's obsession with death is revealed in his *Sonnets*.

Published in *The Assam Tribune*

09

Wintry Sojourns

You beckon me
And I trudge along;
Reluctantly through foggy hills
Driving, swerving, struggling
Through cloud and mist,
As if towards heaven.

Only to discover
A once beautiful, now dirty –
Shillong – Scotland of the East,
The concrete jungle of today,
Yesteryears symbol of peace.
Now, the curfew haven.
A tourist resort, not anymore
Giving way to violence, extortion and thwarted peace
Which here, as elsewhere
Mars every day.

The Christmas sun
Grows bright, mature and pleasant
As I drive along.
It is no holiday
Though Yule-tide is here;
Instead, assignments and deadlines are to be met
Before I can join the cheer.
An unease calm has taken over,

Bloodshed stopped for now,
Mind you, only for now –
To usher in festivity
Calling for celebration,
A celebration – undeserved.

I only wait and watch
Merry shoppers, chirpy and gay,
Amidst the glow and warmth
Of the decorated pine, holly, wreaths and mistletoe;
Forgetting the message of Christ
His pain, suffering and endurance,
With equal numbness, ignoring –
His message of love
The reason behind his death.

The days die
The mercury level drops;
Yet mentor and I,
Over cups of tea
A heater for company,
Spend mornings, afternoons and evenings –
Pouring over issues of power and authority
The fate of women, ages ago
And of one who have struggled, survived,
Trying to show,
And see the path too.

The cold increases,
Another day is gone;
Smog and fog conquer the afternoons,
The weakening rays of the sun –
How I dread this,

Yet I carry on
To colder climes, more dreadful than this,
For the desert capital calls
To the heart of the sub-continent;
To make voices heard,
Those voices I carry from here
The stifled voices of me and my multitude,
Our message, yearnings and aspirations,
Unsure, whether we,
Will be heard.

Fulfil the task I must,
I tell myself;
As I pass through
Crowded planned streets,
Tall buildings, manicured gardens,
Dilapidated relics of the past too,
Here, old and new submerge
Yet, the rough bullish throng, both young and old
Fail to learn
The messages of old
That could have taught, to avoid
Histories repeated mistakes.

The air is authoritarian
Trying to control,
What fails to be controlled –
Minds and spirits, indomitable as before;
False queen, puppet king and courtiers,
Like monarchy of old
Has to learn
Where hearts are not won over
The conquest is always half-won.

The train chugs along,
I return to home and hearth,
To find solace, peace at home
A peace betrayed, away from home.
Yet mind remains restless,
Discontented, disillusioned
As my wintry sojourn
Keeps haunting,
Opening unanswered questions and more,
That I, never can answer,
On my own.

Published in *The Assam Tribune*

10

Birthday

What's a birthday?
I question myself;
Is it a day in a year!
When I, torn out of the womb –
Ripped out from her protective darkness,
Made separate from my mother
Brought into this disquietening light;
Into this cruel world
Teeming with life;
But one that will not let me live!

No, I didn't want to come out,
Had no desire to see all these,
Experience pain and sorrow
That it unfolds,
Into my life;
Nullify my existence,
Stifle my voice,
Kill my spirit –
Try to fit me to a mould.
Chaining me down
With worn-out rituals,
Customs and traditions
That ceases to make sense,

Stultifies my growth
Snuffing me out
While compelling me to carry on.

I did not seek to be born,
To have a birthday
That reminds me,
Every year and every day –
Of the fate of others before me;
Women in attics,
Mad women they were called,
For they did not conform
To rules made by man,
Compelling them to die,
Die every day
Before death actually came;
While some without hope or fear
Committed suicide.

There were a few madmen too,
Very few though
Like Harold Pinter's anti-hero,
Surviving to mourn
His unfortunate Birthday Party –
That transforms him so,
That he is unrecognizable to himself.
Pulled, twisted, mercilessly tortured,
Made finally to yield;
Like a zombie,
Powerless to think,
Immobilized to question.

This is frightening
I dread to be such a one,
Scared to have another birthday
That will dole out death, not life.
No, I want to live
To breathe freely,
To laugh and be merry;
To think, to question, to argue,
Fight for what is mine,
Assert my voice, my opinion,
To let me, be me.

With fears have I lived,
A decade or two,
But hope for a second birth –
A second birthday,
Different from old.
Fears shall be wiped away,
For I have dreams to live,
Do what I want
Unshackled and free,
To grow, tell my story,
Do all these and much more.

11

Sisterhood

I don't know
The meaning of this word
Is it synonymous to 'brotherhood',
To be used in conjunction with it,
Or as a complementary word,
Is it like becoming a member of a club?
What does one do,
To become a part of it?
To be a woman
Is that not enough?
To share food,
Buy groceries together
And, the important shopping too!
Laugh over a burnt curry,
Cry over an empty gas cylinder,
And hug one another?

Yet sisters are worst rivals,
Women caught in jealously –
Manipulating and scheming
Trying to score over the other.
Women beware women
We have been cautioned since long,
Yet we are to learn the lesson
To avoid the sly tricks we play
That we ought to have learned, by now.

We needn't confine to a nunnery,
Abstain from men and company.
Instead, to be in the thick of things,
Renounce cunning to be compassionate,
Give up lies and be accommodating
Attempt, to understand ourselves;
Listen patiently –
To each other's story,
In this can be a sisterhood
That will surpass all brotherhood.

Published in *The Assam Tribune*

12

✦

Missing You

Caught between two worlds
Neither the devil, nor
The deep blue sea
Instead loving, giving
More than I deserve,
Love beyond limitation;
One old, the other new,
Each close to my heart
A part of me
Yet so far apart.

For the two I live,
O, My two worlds
That alone makes sense
In an otherwise meaningless world.
Courage, hope, direction
They unfailingly shower;
Solidly beside me
In joys and sorrows,
Angry in protectiveness,
Balmy in pain,
Ready to fight for me
When in pain.

Similar, despite differences
My two disparate worlds,
Sharing emotions and feelings,
Bound together by a bond,
A bond, that is me;
Physically remote
Geographically inhabiting different climes;
Yet successfully providing me,
In distance or in proximity,
Fruition and completeness.

One nurtured me for decades
From day one till today,
With unflagging love –
Sacrifice untold,
Like a precious pearl
They cocooned me in their oyster,
Made me that I am today.
Love and friendship infinite
Came from them,
With joys unbound
Rolling and playing
As I grew.

The second world have opened
One I inhabit now,
Affecting new emotions
Hitherto unknown,
From one who rules my heart,
My friend, my lover,
Partner in life and more,

Holding promises for tomorrow –
Promises to bring,
My two worlds
Soon united together.

Yet today I miss
That which is torn from me,
For now –
When I am with one
The other is always far apart.

13

Milieu

Is this what I had expected to see!
Do not tell me,
That this is it!
I had hoped to find beauty
Past grandeur, glory and stateliness;
Instead to be greeted
By staleness and stagnation,
Witness a fear to change;
We all hate change,
But here is –
Reluctance to grow, to see, to adopt.

An ancient culture
Caught in its web,
A once past glory,
Now reeling in its shadow.
Caught in superstition
Malpractices, caste, dowry –
Systems once convenient,
Made growth possible and sense,
Now redundant and decayed
Still rules the day.

Stubborn in conservativeness,
Orthodox in practices,

Still harbouring the old theory –
Of women's inferiority to men
The need to subdue,
To govern, to command, to control,
Absolving adultery
Almost legitimizing it –
Only for men!
Nurturing this terrible wrong,
In this age
When women have reached space.

I see around mothers and sisters chained down,
To centuries ago,
It is all in their mind though
Effectively, psychologically,
Cutting them down,
With long plaits like chains
Women pulling women down,
Fulfilling so called societal roles.
The five-metre sari too
The anklets that tinkle with it
Meant to adorn
But actually holding them down
Like cuffs, restricting their stride
Arresting their flights of fancy,
All are meant
To cut them down.

Yet things are moving ahead –
Going fast too,
In another direction though,
A giant on its stride
Mechanically, uncomprehendingly,

Towards a direction
A techies mechanical world,
Where technology is honoured,
Freedom and creativity –
Ignored.

I look around – an outsider,
Insignificant, withdrawn,
Scared at the prospect
Of becoming a part of it.
I know it will not leave me untouched,
It is all strange to me today,
Yet a day will soon come
When it shall be a part of me.

I see around
Dirt, filth and decay,
Poverty, illiteracy, ignorance,
Rudeness, lies, deceit, corruption,
Fidelity that got lost,
A thousand things more
Crying out
Desperately, in need to break loose,
But most of all –
The minds
Our thoughts reborn.

Visions of change
Meets my eyes,
Juxtaposed with the grace of Bharatanatyam
The sweet notes of classical music
Drifting like oasis in a desert,
Scattered and weak

Way and far away;
Too far, are the voices of change
To make its presence felt,
The muffled voices –
Remain mostly unheard,
Amidst this opposing stream of things.

How long will it remain so,
Refusing itself to change;
Continue to stiffly oppose
The winds of change –
When the world is moving one way,
How can it afford to move –
In another way.
In this manner
How long shall it carry on,
When will it be ready to accept change.
Wake Up – Wake Up – Wake Up
My people
And, lead the way.

Night to Night Again

Is it the beginning of a new day,
Or the last few hours
Of the one that is about to end?
Surely, it is past the ghostly hour
The cock has not yet crowed,
We venture out
Impulsive you may call,
To be lost –
Over fun, dance and drinks,
The dizzying smoke
On the dance floor,
Where girls barely clad,
Shake breasts and hips.

This is not an escape
We repeatedly convince ourselves,
No, we are not disillusioned
Nor, caught in ennui,
We are happy
But seek to be gay.
Whom do we deceive?
Ourselves!
For we know not
What is happiness,
Thus, merely try to be gay.

Riches, success and fashion,
Spiritualism too,
Is a style statement
That one carries
Like an evening bag
Thank God! There is money
Which promises to fill the void,
Never to let down
Even when other promises fail.

Late nights, pubs and discos,
Followed by caffeine
To do away the blues;
We wake up again
To find ourselves –
For the stale day
Has already made its way.

The daily rigmarole begins,
Our return –
To sweet nothingness
To a mental stalemate
To bitch, to the rat race
To all that fails fulfilment;
Only awaiting our return
To dim lights
The tingling of ice-cubes against glass
To drown ourselves
In another dizzying night.

Published in *The Assam Tribune*

15

Being Lonely

I have often heard
People talk of loneliness,
Not just the ordinary you(s) and I(s)
But great ones too,
For it is often lonely at the top
Executives, bankers, business tycoons
As also wives, husbands, lovers
And, many a children too.

I have often seen
Loneliness –
In false smiles
At fashionable parties,
Over cocktails and cigarettes
Held between red painted nails;
In a lonely figure walking distraught,
Carrying a hint of fear
Desperately trying to hide it though –
The prostitute trudging along.

In those bedrooms
Where wives and husbands,
Fail to control their tears;
For although at elbow's length

They are a world apart.
The child too,
Weeps inside his blanket,
Prey to drugs and crimes
Attempting to overcome his misery,
Learns how miserably it fails,
Dragging him down, instead.

Tales of loneliness
Buzz around,
Both inside and outside marriages
As a spouse awaits return –
In a hopeless desire to share a moment,
That rather than bringing them close
Pulls them further away.
It does its round
With a ditched lover
In his frantic wait for the phone to ring;
And as children fall asleep
Cold and lonely,
While their busy mothers toil far away.

I have often heard
Of loneliness in a crowd,
Where surrounded by multitude
Yet none to call one's own.
It is a threatening darkness
That attempts to engulf me too,
Beyond a psychological state –
Instead swallow me
On mornings, evenings and nights,
As the world around gets busy,
And I am lonely and on my own,

With only the green walls of the house
Surrounding me,
That sucks my life out.

Published in *The Assam Tribune*

*   Minor changes have been included in this poem from the
      published version.

16

Varanasi

Your Ghats as beautiful as of old
But today
Beside weeps a river
Lo behold!
The poor Ganges
Worshipped as Goddess
A symbol of purity
Revered with lamps and flowers,
Yet she begs to let her survive,
To be spared from
Sewage, foetuses and ashes of the dead.
In a world
That is truly irreverential,
Where even pure Ganges
Fails to purify Herself.

Varanasi and Ganges
Brethren of old
Of good times and all
Whispering Hindu rites and rituals
To one another
O! how Hinduism is incomplete
Without one or the other!
Seat of our ancient civilization
Witness to its genesis, growth and decay.

Revered Kasi
Renowned since old,
A centre of learning,
Of religion and culture, too –
Even today
Which pulls us all to you.
Yet when we visit
This mighty soul of old
One is greeted
With stains of spit and shit galore
Competing with one another
Who can colour
The streets more.

Here poverty rules the roost,
Corruption breeds
In ancient temples,
Amongst the priests;
Also, beyond –
Among street sellers, autowallas, hotel clerks,
Among those unable to write their names
The claws of poverty extends too
Making of each a victim,
All ultimately a part of the system
Where many are unable to wield the pen.

Irony, shall we say
For Kasi of all
Famed for its great varsity of old
Yet, here by the thousands
Are lives –
Spent in ignorance, poverty and filth

With spirituality almost as good as dead.
O! Varanasi when shall you wake up again,
Can you revive your grandeur of old?

Published in The Assam Tribune

*   Based on my visit to Benaras in 2006. Changes have been brought
      about some 15 years later. Their effectiveness, I am yet to witness.

17

The Red River

You are the son of god,
Aren't you Brahmaputra called?
O! The son of the Creator among gods
Yet more often than not,
You a mindless destroyer,
Ironically, you are the Red River called –
Red not from blood
But the colour of the earth.
Is it just a name,
Or, are you O Majestic One
Truly the son of the immortal one?
Be that as it may
You, the master of floods and furies –
Is also the life giving one.

The only man of a river
In a country full of female ones
Among the Ganga, Yamuna and Cauverys
You are the only Brahmaputra;
You the patriarch
Through and through a man
Handsome, imposing and bold –
Reckless in love;

A traveller, like the mighty conquerors of old,
Climbing down the Himalayas
Crossing rugged terrains
Stretching yourself in valleys,
An adventurer at heart.
Yet like an old man
After all exploits are over
You seek peace and oblivion
As if, a long day is brought to a close.

Merging with the sea
You love to loose yourself
To become one totally different,
Flirting with rivers and tributaries,
After all your hectic adventures
Through three countries
Diverse people and races,
It is difficult to belief,
You give away your guarded identity
Those identities, you have changed cleverly
Like a spy,
From country to country.

For centuries, you are the father
Nay, not a mother
For with joys you have given as much tears
Life with one hand,
Floods and torrents with the other –
To those loyal, subservient and obedient
You awe and inspire;
Despite all pains and losses
You, we love and admire

Now and always
We remain your dependent,
Wish that you, and only you
Be our elixir.

Published in *Eclectic*

18

The Story of Us

I am educated
Cultured and intelligent too;
Have a career
With a mind of my own too;
Yes, I am 'the modern woman'
Dress, speak and carry myself
In this style too;
I drive, swim and tango,
Besides, score on the billiard table too;
Can hold a drink, smoke a cigar,
Debate and put my point through;
I make myself belief
I can do everything
A man can do.

Yet I feel
I am ancient,
Carrying the burden of women
Thousands of years old –
Bound by all those stale rules and dead traditions
That have chained them then,
And holds me down now.

Am I any better today?
Will my fate change tomorrow?

How has my education helped?
I ask myself –
How has a job
Made me any different
From women hundreds of years ago?

Do I not continue
Fulfilling all those chores
That my predecessors have been doing
Since centuries old?
I cook, wash and scrub
Like them
Change nappies and breast feed too.
Look after my husband,
Make his bed
And wash his plates too.
Additionally, I am burdened
With e-mails and calls,
Assignments and researches too
As my mind also plays
What curry to cook.
I clear the table, wash clothes,
While he, my better half
Lolls on the sofa –
Playing a mobile game or two,
And calls it a day.

Is the family only mine;
My responsibility –
I ask myself again;
To obey hubby, raise kids and
Make in-laws happy
Will forever be my bane.

How can I not see myself
A thousand years old
Burdened with that have been their's –
And a lot more;
A gift or curse
Of financial independence and education
I am too tired to know.

19

Fidelity

God knows!
I always wanted to trust you,
Had indeed, trusted you –
A trust that love breeds;
Till the fine thread
Threatened to break,
And almost did snap,
Over things said and unsaid,
In one spring.

You know better than I –
Trust and loyalty
Are bosom friends,
In love, marriage and all relationships.
"Frailty, thy name is woman"
Shakespeare had said,
Yet today I beg to differ
O! Wish instead,
To speak for women
For all those who have been betrayed
Their stories unsaid.

Come, shall we now talk
Of men's frailty –
Promises, made to be broken,
Of this bitter reality –

Try how much we want
We cannot erase.

Today, I plead –
Do not promise again,
No, not another vow on me;
For I fear –
One more carelessness
On your part,
Might cost me dear.
O! how could I not see,
Trusting blindly, blindly indeed,
Failed to see those hints,
I should have deciphered.

Relationships are deceived,
Over matters big and small.
Ties as old as you,
Parents and brothers
Connections of blood;
O! How is it possible,
That you be
True to one,
And, only one
So unlike your fellow brothers…

20

Monsoon Mournings

Ah! Monsoon is here
Those very special mornings,
Bringing memories of Tagore's *Geetanjali*
Refreshing me, as I look around –
The earth rejuvenated, fresh and green
Ready to speak;
Flowers sparkling with raindrops,
Dust settled,
Life young, new and full of vigour
Seems to blend in perfect harmony;
That decades ago
Gurudev* connected so very perfectly
Seeking soul's unification with God
In this mother of a season.

My favourite season of the year
Will you refresh me too,
Wipe away like dust,
All my sorrows from the past?
Pleasure! the day has made a cloudy start
Drizzling, ready to burst,
Look, it speaks the language of my heart.
Mourning, set to break in torrents –
The day and I are ready
To refresh memories

Of bygone hurts,
Wounds healed long ago
But alas, they still seem to cut!

After all, is this not monsoon!
Promising a fresh lease of life
Or, is it just rejuvenation for earth and plants
And not of mere mortal, me.
With sorrows old and new,
Endeavour my spirits to rise
After all, its a new morn
A new day and season,
Only to find the weeping season reliving
Not Tagore's spirituality
But floods and furies around,
And for me a deluge –
Overflowing my heart.

*   Rabindranath Tagore was also lovingly known as 'Gurudev', meaning – the teacher, because of his immense contribution to liberal education

21

Writer's Block

Writers do not speak of it,
While artists shy away from it
And geniuses shun it –
Some of them even agree
This vacuum of creativity
Do not exist.
Yet Shakespeare
Went through it,
Experienced this totally unpoetic
Fearing, wishing, hoping
This would forever
Stay away from him.

Yet today I explore
This most unpoetic of unpoetic,
Is it because
For want of a topic
I have chosen 'writer's block'?
I intend to mock it,
Though I cannot shoo it away,
For me as for many –
It is a reality
No matter how much we wish
We cannot do away.

I am no Marquez,
Unlike him
Will not die
If I do not write;
A void at the most will feel,
An aspiration unrealized,
Fulfilment lacking
Depression may rise.

Yet I will not talk of it,
With fellow comrades of the trade!
A guarded secret it will be,
Kept away from family and friends!
Instead act a front –
Will put up a show of brilliance:
Be busy without business,
In bored drawl
Will deliberate on learned topics,
All there is
From culture to politics;
Till writer's block dissipates away
And I can, once again
Wield the pen.

Published in *Eclectic*

22

Farewell

The moment
To bid farewell
Is here. This day,
God knows, I have infinitely tried
To delay, push it back –
From one day to the other;
Even though, almost sure was I,
That there be no glimmer of hope
To crown my efforts.

Cruel irony, it is,
That farewell I bid,
Same time of the year
When exactly ten years ago –
As a new bride,
I entered expectantly –
A new world
Brimming with hope,
With love and promises;
Dreaming to make a home.
Never, never
Did I know then,
Ten years hence,
An unfortunate farewell
Lay in store.

Ten long years
Have I borne,
Where every day has taken a toll,
Wearing me, breaking me down
In ways, undreamt of.
Yet today, the rush of emotions
Flood over,
With meagre control,
As I bid farewell
To the house,
That I had made a home,
To nooks and corners –
Loads of memories –
Nurtured and cherished,
Things dear to me
Which dear might remain
For all years to come
In very different circumstances.

Fate has made a mockery
Of this unfortunate finale,
Where with little time to mourn,
Thoughts running berserk,
The day rushes by –
In a maze of hectic activities,
In gathering pieces of my life
Packing in suitcases –
Ten years of my life,
Nay, unpacking my life;
Taking with me,
Memories, responsibilities,
Children of mine,

And of him
Who was once mine.

Is there a point
In questioning destiny's cruel joke?
Wisdom perhaps lies,
In comprehending every bit,
The immensity of loss –
Reputation tarnished –
Years wasted –
Emotions lost –
Health and wealth injured –
Damages never to be undone –
Culminating in a farewell,
A fitting end
To an unfitting episode.

23

Sixty Years of Independence

O, what hype and fanfare!
Don't you know
Today is India's sixtieth Independence Day.
Crackers burst,
An English snack is cut,
Look, look
A greedy *neta** devours the cake first!

O, such celebrations!
Don't you know
India is an economic super power now?
An enthusiast nudges
And adds, why you forget
A military super power of today.

I look around –
Towns and cities
Guarded by the military
For fear lurks
That a militant's bomb may spurt,
And snatch another commoner away.
Suddenly my pace is stalled,
To let a convoy pass,
A fleet of two and twenty cars –
Singled out in uniformity

Pointed guns their only character,
Shielding a minister –
Do not mistake,
A no commoner is he.

A little further
Young crowds rush,
Slaves of foreign culture
In minis and leather stuff,
For a glitzy hip up-market club.
While others flock to designer malls
Spending thousands on an I-pod,
Over boutique drinks, branded outfits
Trying to acquire a little class,
Oblivious, that at the entrance
Begs an underage mother,
For her skinny infant son.

News channels suddenly flash –
Dead bodies
Of thirteen school going lads,
But the jaded crowd carries on
Unmoved, unperturbed
By this common incident
Of a bomb blast.
And why not?
Something interesting is happening,
As metros and cities reel under man-made floods.

An old farmer cries
All his produce lost to flood,
No, he is not the only one
Thousand others cry,

While some choose death with a wry smile –
For those millions of hectares
Of crops,
That devastated lie.

Where are India's new millionaires,
The corporate moguls and high-tech barons,
The eager politicians with empty promises,
Who now are busy filling their pockets?
Mother India weeps
With the old skeleton farmer,
The underage mother,
The unfed and the illiterate,
The girl-child killed inside the womb,
For the wife burnt to death.
For the real India
That is still unchanged;
Forgotten conveniently for the present,
As India basks
In her sixtieth anniversary of independence.

*   neta – colloquial for politician

24

The Unattainable

Of you and I,
Our story,
Of our involvement in a search –
Yesterday, today and tomorrow
Engaged in that silent pursuit
An eternal wait,
For that special
That yearning destined to remain
Forever and forever
The unattainable.

It promises ultimate fulfilment
Joy and happiness,
Never to be known
Never to be experienced,
The unattainable since it eternally remains,
Changing its meanings
From you to me,
Still for each of us
The thing
Closest to our heart.

For the orphan,
Could it be
The mother she will never have?

No matter how much she yearns
It is the thing
She can never get.
While for some
It is a child which she will never have.

Yet there are those
Whose unattainable remains elusive,
Unknown and not understood –
Is it the goal
We will never reach
Only to be dreamt
To aspire for
Elusive and effervescent
More beautiful and dear
Beyond wildest imagination.

Our attainable happiness;
The love of a spouse
Which we desire and get
But never enough
Not to our fulfilment,
This love and care
No matter how much
In this case!

It is no shadow
Over-casting our lives,
A mere little hint of sadness
To garnish our whiles,
Like the occasional drizzle
Suddenly it comes,

Now and then,
To leave behind
An emotion
A promise of bliss
Not easy to forget.

25

Caged Kings

An object of pity now,
But once a feared king –
Mighty, majestic beast
Lord of the forest
Hero of tales, myths and legends
Yet here you are bound,
Away from home
In a cage,
Not six feet asunder.

Old, diseased, partly blind
Enfeebled by your restricting confines,
Discarded,
No longer of use,
Too weak to jump –
Through rings of fire,
Play circus tricks
The ordinary populace
Foolish, laughing and jeering
Loves to see,
The king
Play the jester,
For the joy of the crowd.

Those days are bygones
When you,
A circus lion,
Would take instructions
From the clown.
Now, the electric rod
Budges you not,
Thus, you are left
Thirsty and underfed,
To die a thousand deaths
In the blazing sun,
A mere shadow, broke inside out.

Whose burden are you?
The question crops –
The master of gimmicks
Shrug their shoulders,
Strongly denying,
How can it be?
Since of no use now
They staunchly refuse
That to you they owe.

While those in dreary offices,
Sitting in shabby towelled chairs
Behind the official logo and crest,
With no time to spare –
Mutters lethargically
In their attempt
To skirt the topic,
That the paperwork is so great
It is not worth the case.

Poor victim of fate
Once a king
Now worse than a beggar
Without a choice
Refused even
The choice of death
I pity us, not you
For doing
Which we should
NEVER, NEVER, NEVER
Have done to you!

26

My Lost Self

Who am I?
Am I me? I ask myself –
I look at the shadow of my former self,
Searching for that lost spirit
That lived zestful days.

Yet here I am,
Merely a shadow of myself;
An anonymous soul
In an anonymous place,
An outcast –
Amidst a multitude,
Unknown, unrecognized, unappreciated
A faceless presence
Among the teeming populace.

Lost in direction,
In this bustling metro,
Seeking to find a home
A home that cannot be;
Neighbours here are many,
People and some company –
Of different hues and attitude
But none
To call my own.

Love, compassion, fellow feeling,
Seem to belong
To an unreachable past;
Unbelievable though it may seem,
Surrounded as I am
By my own,
Whom I had thought –
Are now holding back from me.

Living amidst oblivion,
Should I give up –
The search for my former self?
Relegate to a distant past,
Dream of a lost world,
Loose myself among that opium happiness
Promising further unhappiness.

Accept and agree,
Should I, my lost identity?
Renounce the search for self,
Create and be content –
Forcefully adjust
With an inferior half-self,
Unrenewed, unrejuvenated
A mere impression of my lost self.

27

❦

Soul

My soul,
Neither lost, nor newly found –
Had really no story to tell,
Of interest,
Or, to ponder upon,
Like yours, was mine,
It lay dormant
– Somewhere,
Knew it existed,
Took it for granted
Seldom giving it a thought.

My soul,
Really, did not need to be searched
Lay quiet in deep slumber
– Somewhere…
Waking occasionally,
To take a peek
Only to return snuggly
To an unending nap,
As if, it were dead.
There was no time
Was a handy excuse,
To spare my soul
A minute or two,
Have a tête-à-tête

Whisper something
Trivial or meaningful.

My soul,
Its story
Like yours,
Excuse me, if I may say so
Was struggling –
To keep pace
In a frenzied friendless world,
Unable to grip
The maddening flurry
At home and at work,
Where materialism took over
Love, and everything else
Worth living for,
My soul, instead
Chose to ignore it all,
For peace,
To be had in undisturbed sleep.

My soul,
Years later,
At the very threshold of a new journey
Into another world –
Of no return,
Might, look back,
At its long uneventful journey
Where, it stirred not a soul
And, in turn
Remained muted,
Living
A life equal to death.

28

Gift of Spirituality

Spiritualism, her very embodiment
Lies deep and quiet
In her heart and soul,
Of this ancient country
Bharatvarsha, Hindustan or India
As she is called;
This hallowed land
Mother of spirituality,
Fountainhead of wisdom –
Millenniums old.

Revered is *The Gita*
That sprang from her bosom,
Invaluable the *Vedic* philosophies,
The Upanishads,
Worth their value in gold;
Spreading the light of truth,
Quenching the thirst of seekers,
Of *Rishis, munis, sanyasis, dasis**,
As among the layman
And foreign brethren
In distant shores,
Whom her spiritual soul
Has embraced as her own.

Sathyam Shivam Sundaram[1]
Remains the eternal truth;
Maharishi Vishwamitra's *Gyatri Mantra*[2],
Shastras[3] from the greatest minds of yore;
Handed down to generations
Revealing the path of bliss and salvation;
Buddha, Mahavira – her worthiest sons
Spoke words of purest philosophy
Enriching *Bharatvarsha's* spiritual soul
Lifting her out of prejudices
When she needed them the most;
While *Sufi* saints and *Baul* singers[4]
Carried across her length and breadth,
Message of love and brotherhood
Traversing boundaries, religions and states.

Thousands of years have passed,
Endless generations
Born and re-born,
Mankind still turns to *Bharatvarsha's* spirituality –
The need for her ancient spiritual wisdom
As fervent as before,
Seeking direction, seeking enlightenment;
Throughout humanity's history,
And even now,
In pursuit of peace and solace
Returning, again and again
To the *Vedas* and *Upanishads*
To, the wisdom of *The Gita*.

O! The land of the Himalayas and the Ganga,
Of *The Ramayana* and *The Mahabharata,*
Of *Shaivism, Vaishnavism* and *Tantricism*[5]

This is the soil that nurtured
Merging these rivers of knowledge
In a single confluence
Making the deepest ocean
Huge and eternal as the cosmos,
Answering humanity's undying quest
Through this *amritam*[6] of knowledge
That transcends ordinary understanding
Lifting mankind to the extraordinary
To the sublime.

[*] Wise men of the old, sages, devotees
[1] An ancient Hindu saying, meaning truth, godliness and beauty
[2] According to Hindu legend the once powerful King Vishwamitra who later went on the become a renowned sage, conceived this verse, which has remained immensely popular till date.
[3] Ancient texts
[4] Devotional singers from Islam and Hindu religion, who were more secular and less orthodox; they preferred to see the image of God through love for their fellow human beings.
[5] Different sects of Hinduism
[6] The divine nectar or drink of the gods, which as myth goes, promises immortality; generally speaking it refers to a taste of the divine.

29

—❖—

Experiencing the Divine

The cool wind across my face,
The stray rays –
Of the first morning sun
Frolicking with big shady trees,
Harmonizing light and shade
With peace and quietude,
Its precious embellishments;
A twittering here,
A fluttering there,
A stray dog or two;
Soul and nature
At this divine moment –
Joining as one,
Lifts up in gratitude
Full of joy and praise
To the Creator, the Almighty,
To Blessed Nature!

In God-inspiring beginnings as these –
A heavy heart lightens
And, if only for a moment,
The mind elates
Leaving behind existential worries
In this magical ambience.
Brightening up the saddest soul,
Which has forgotten –
The meaning of rejoice.

In a corner
Sheltered by trees
But not from human eyes,
Lies a small temple
Closed,
The deity within fast asleep
Awaiting to be awakened –
With holy mantras
The priest shall chant
As he rings the bell
Offering flowers with prayers.

The dawn is perfect
Is complete,
This the divine
The experience –
Is yet short-lived,
As the sun brightens
The day matures,
As folks set about their chores,
Yet like the fragrance of a flower
This experience lingers
Throughout the day,
Wafting its reassuring promise,
That sheer peace and beauty
Shall revive once more,
When the mind and soul –
In another crack of dawn,
Shall again reach out
At that precise moment
In the glory of the Lord!

30

A Single-Handed Experience

My single-handed experience
Real not fictional,
Is literary, single handed
I did say.
Yet another phase
Has descended on me,
Where within a span of years
At regular intervals,
When forced I am to struggle
Day after day and weeks in a row
Work, eat and sleep,
Literary, with just one hand.

Bound is my other hand
Very tightly,
Without an inch to move
Strapped to my body
Fated to live this ordeal
For twenty-one days flat.
Not a day less
Not a day more
When every movement is a struggle
Every day – endless.

Dependent I am
On my dear ones
And on those,
Who are neither near, nor dear
A blow to independent me
Which now of necessity
Have to bow,
To receive a helping-hand
That comes from far and near.

A spectacle I have become,
Attracting curious looks
Of passer-bys, on-lookers,
Who attempts to figure out
The single-handed spectacle
That I am now.

31

The Silence of Sita

Have I wondered why?
Filled with awe
About stories of the statue of gold,
A statue that sat next to Ram
And how a statue could ever suffice…
Replace the wife of flesh and blood
As he performed the feared Ashwamedha Yajya*
To conquer realms and kingdoms – uncontested
After conquering the hearts of all.

A statue of gold – spoke of wealth,
As also of his loyalty to Sita
His love,
Refusing to marry again
To replace, his loving wife,
Who followed him
Without conditions and expectations
Far and wide.

Yet that day, it was this unforgettable gold statue
Sitting quiet, speaking volumes
Of all that formed her, moulded her…
Tied her, crushed her and finally buried her,
Of norms and ethos, customs and traditions,
That required only her silent statue
Nothing more…

In rituals grand, enormous
Made by men, and for them,
To firmly establish men as lords.

What was allowed of her?
As a woman,
To remain silent, not utter
Or, ever mutter the holy verses,
Those sacred verses,
Which were the haloed domain
Of men – of only a privileged few!

No wonder her statue alone would suffice,
Her presence, her words…
Not important, not required
Might instead give rise to embarrassment
Maybe even discontent,
So, only a dumb and mum
Statue would do just as good!
Never ask questions, or demand answers,
Destined to remain Silent Forever.

*   A religious ceremony that established the undisputed rule of a
monarch

Published online in *Guwahati Grand Poetry Festival* (GGPF) in July
2021

32

Song of the Butterfly

O butterfly, beautiful butterfly,
Evoked,
By poets, painters, artists and authors,
Who sing your peans
Loves to imagine you as work of art
Epitome of beauty
Symbol of transformation
Of what was and what can be…

Exquisite, ethereal, weightless and fancy
Have we ever thought of your pain
Pain of metamorphosis?
Did you wish to change, did they ever ask?
Perhaps you were happier lazing around
Nibbling on a leaf in your original state;
Liked to remain hidden,
With no aspirations to fly
Or, contest in beauty pageants
Amongst insects wild.

Did they see your pain…
Feel the fragility of your powdery wings
Delicate, vulnerable, yet so pretty…
As you laboured from flower to flower
To collect nectar.

Made to breed, to lay
All but to be achieved
In short two weeks?

Gone are the days
When you loved to merely crawl
Under a cool shade or in the sun;
Now you cannot even run
But must fly,
Do the impossible
In an impossibly short time…
Before you rest forever
Often pregnant with eggs and full,
Overburdened – you age too swiftly and die.

Your pain, your struggle, your lack of rest
Your tiredness
We never see –
We only capture
But what our eyes can see
Just your flitting beauty… not your heavy heart,
As you bring joy, spread smiles
While within, your pain survives.

Published online in *Guwahati Grand Poetry Festival* (GGPF) in Jan. 2022

33

The Record Player

Time is but a memory
A memory – that never dies
A faded photographic memory
Long forgotten in the recesses of time,
Until suddenly one day
It flashes back in all clarity.
Time recreates memory
Of bygone era
Our forefathers', and here of
My grandfather's record player

It looked queer to my childish eyes,
I think it was a square big box
That sat cozy in the drawing room corner
With slim records to give it company
And together they would create quite a buzz, a flurry
Enliven dull moments
Ausage the pain of a broken heart.

Lazy summer afternoons whiled away
As Rabindra Sangeet it played
Or, on spirited evenings when one twisted and stepped
To the tune of Hindi melodies
Kishore Kumar or Lata
His Master's Voice would always oblige
Who can forget the unforgettable picture

Of the mindful, alert dog
Peeked up and eager, to obey and please.

But, the cassette player arrived
Orange, bright and portable
From American shores by an aunt close-by,
The record-player gradually lay forgotten
The records gathering dust
No longer played
Bringing smiles and joys
But itself cut a sorry picture
Of being old and bored
Till one day, shifted away
In the dark corner, of a little used room.

Clothes, sweaters, towels, all things sundry
Were heaped on it
Till it was pushed further away
To the storeroom,
Where it lay still
Un-played, unheard for many years
Untold, forgotten
The records were moth eaten
Just as it was
Until finally it was thrown out
As a garbage to be brunt
With moth eaten photographs, mother's moth-eaten guitar
Discarded… Gone…
Never remembered, never missed,
Never to tune again.

34

What Is...?

What is it to love
What is it to cry
What is it to laugh
What is it to die
What is it to be born
What is it to live
What is it to get, and
What is it to give.

What is it to forget
What is it to forgive
What is it to mingle
What is it to be single
What is it to feel
What is it to unfeel
What is it to rise
What is it to fall
What is it to lie
What is it to jump
What is it to dive
What is it to jive...

What is it to grow
What is it to shrink
What is it to run

What is it to blink
What is it to be alone
What is it to brood
What is it to eat
What is it to starve?

What is it to sleep
What is it to be awake.
What is it to think
What is it to ask
What is it to seek
What is it to question, and
What is the answer?

What is this life
What is this gaze
What is this view
What is this haze
What is the path
Where is the way?
A million question dawns and fades
What is, What if and What might be.

35

Right & Wrong

You say, you are right
He says, she is wrong
She says, this is right
Someone else says, that is wrong
What is right …
And, what is wrong?
A wise one said
They are but,
Two sides of the same coin.

Right to you
Feels wrong to me
-Is matter of perception
Difference of opinion
Different approach
Of looking at the same thing.
Any wonder then,
An enemy –
Is a patriot for the other side;
A thief is a provider too...
All smudged grey and blue
What is right for me, dear
Is not so right for you.

Stories are one-sided
History tells but half-truths
Perhaps, even less
Just the truth of one side
While wrong done to the other
Is hidden
Indeed, pushed aside.

We hear the victorious
But what happens to the losers,
We hear male voices
But what about the female ones,
Voices of the oppressor speak
Hushed away, are the oppressed multitude.

How can I any longer believe
How right is right
Or, that wrong is wrong;
Not question
Right from wrong,
Not question stories that has been told,
Blindly accept and believe
What has been said as –
Right and Wrong.

36

Tiger, Tiger!

"Tyger Tyger, burning bright,
*In the forests of the night;"**

Tiger, tiger …
Tells a different story today…
Are you still feared?
Do you still burn bright?
Or, do you hide in fear
Away from the human eye.

To catch your glimpse
Many covet,
In your protected habitat,
In Manas, we were told,
Is where to find.
Yet in the same refrain, is informed
That only a very lucky few
Gets a glimpse,
Or at best, footprints –
Left behind.

Today, your highness, your royal breed
Numbers to a pathetic few …
A mere double digit

At the same –
Serene, dense and lush abode
Where once you roamed
Proud, feared and free,
Now totally at our mercy
At the hands of greedy humanity,
Not sure if you will make it
To the next century,
Reduced from a hunter
To a prey.

* The opening line of William Blake's *The Tyger*.

Written in memory of my visit to Manas National Park in the winter of 2021.

37

The Clarion Call

We were different
From those before us
And those after,
Like any other generation, I guess
Yet we knew not…
It takes an outsider or an outside
To open our eyes,
To tell you
This is not the normal.
This is not how it was,
Or, will be.

This is about the clarion call
The call that would be made –
That none dare disobey,
The word would spread like wild-fire
It was a tradition,
Not a thing new –
Most normal for us
As we understood
As we knew.

For us,
Far-flung in a corner
Of a huge country,

Almost a continent,
When little recognized,
Understood or appreciated
The state revolted
Wishing to break free
Of a mother, that no longer cared.

Thus, came the revolt
The uprising
The strike back,
But to us, our generation
We were simply too young
To understand, act or react.

To us, were unknown
Republic or Independence Days
It was just another holiday!
But unlike, we were not to step out,
To keep to ourselves
Within the four walls
As the clarion call had been made
*Bandh** announced
As all celebrations
Stood boycotted.

Yet we got glimpses from the telly
Of celebrations in distant Delhi
Or, on occasions when away on travel
Saw fleeting images of
Local gathering,
Students parading in *gullies**1
To the tune of martial beats
Of people moving around as usual

Meeting for some *adda**²*
Taking a stroll.

Yet we were special
Our experiences unique
Lending depth to our understanding, gradually
Of what was, and what could be…
Of what went wrong
Of a path to find
And, where to draw the line –
So that our future generations
Gets a normal life.

Yet no regrets,
For we and our experiences
Are truly special
The clarion call that once was loud
Will remain forever unforgotten
Fresh and etched on memories,
Every year, on every national day.

*   *Bandh* – a call for boycott
*1   *gullies* – by-lanes
*2   adda – a casual gathering of a few, usually in the corner of a roadside, or a small tea-shop

38

Tale of Pondicherry

You remind me of twins
Separated at birth,
Born together, but with time
Became so different and distinct
As not to recognize the other.

One became the 'White Town' –
The French Quarters
As quipped in fashionable circles
Lined with clean avenues, colourful bungalows
Indeed, a pretty French village,
With charming cafes, handsome boutiques,
French style houses
Now converted into cozy hotels
A favourite with tourists
Where wine flows
Music plays
The young and the rich
Dance, shop, wine and dine
Enjoy crepes
Catch-up over some Tart Tartin*.

Side by side
Lies the other town
No, it is not called the 'Brown Town'
Or 'Indian Quarters' or 'Tamil Ville'

It is just another ordinary town
With no fancy cafes lining the lanes and by-lanes
No boutiques, no French style hotels,
Rarely a tourist comes here;
For, vaccy lies in search
Of the unique, the extraordinary
For that is the crux of a journey,
Our feeble attempt to escape the mundane
Shy away from the boredom of life – the everyday.

The talk is not of the tourist,
Of journeys, vacations and destinations
But of two towns
Two sisters, who couldn't be more different from the other
Of wealth and poverty,
Of bias and prejudice
Of rulers and ruled
Of colonizers and colonized
Of suppressor and suppressed
Of (should I say) superior and inferior
Of extraordinary and ordinary
Of domination and subdued
Of two cultures, two languages,
But one existence.

*   A classic French dessert comprising of sweet short crust pastry
and topped with caramelized apples

39

A Note on War

This is not in defense of war
It is not about taking sides
By the way, who are we
Commoners, to take sides
How much do we know
What is our inside knowledge
To jump into a bandwagon
Point out finger and say,
You, my dear friend is right
And you,
On the other side
Must be penalized.

True, there is the humanitarian aspect
Shouting, loud and clear,
We cannot ignore;
We cannot but feel sorry
For the widows, the orphans
The emotionally injured
Or, the physically maimed.

But then,
Isn't that the legacy of war.
Had the much-touted correct side
Prevented this,
Had it been their initiation

There can be no answers
Only a silent prayer
That men be less greedy
Those in power
Learn the language of love
Be *Humane* to one another.

40

Unsung: The Koel Cries

I hear her sweet voice,
Mornings, afternoons and evenings,
At dawn, even before I open my eyes
On hot dry afternoons
Sweet its sounds to the human ear...
Methinks, is it a song,
Or, is it a cry?

With parched thirsty throat
Rendering note after note
Is it singing a happy song...
I fear, I can only hear its pain
No joy
Crying for its new born
In another nest
In someone else's home.

Do I hear the pain of a mother –
Who is not a mother
Has none to call her own –
No children or family,
It is the cry of solitude
But it does not wipe away the pain,
The thirst remains, forever, unquenched,
Yearning for love, family and nest.

The cry of the koel
Haunts day and night,
Refusing to go away,
Leaving a feeling of its overwhelming pain
Perhaps, staining her thirsty throat with blood
From crying hoarse,
Such a sweet voice
Carries only pain
A cursed life
Living a cursed fate.

41

Draupadi

Draupadi…
The name has an ancient ring
A very familiar one
For who hasn't heard
Of the famous wife
A wife with five husbands!
The Draupadi of *The Mahabharata*
Wife, princess, queen and mother
An object of beauty, courage, pride
But above all a woman –
So strong, and so unique,
She towered above the rest…

I also remember of another Draupadi…
By the way, a much coveted name,
Amongst tribals many.
You ask "Why?" –
I know not,
Maybe to draw a link
Connect with a culture past,
As ancient as the tribes
Sharing deep roots with the land.

This Draupadi, none other than
Mahasweta Devi's '*Draupadi*'*

Dopdi Mejhen, as her kinsmen called
Unable to utter,
The Sanskrit way.
Dopdi is Draupadi,
No object of beauty, is she
But a Santhal rebel, a dreaded Naxalite
Much feared,
Of such mettle, that it shook the ground
From beneath the General...
She feared none,
But was dreaded by all
Dopdi laid her life for a cause,
For her tribe, for the forests
And for her roots.

Years and decades later,
Came another Draupadi of renown –
Draupadi Murmu[*1]
A tribal, and a Santhal too
Like, her famed predecessor,
Who rose to become
India's first tribal President
By sheer grit and hard work
From the poorest poor.
Rewriting history,
Completing the circle
Connecting past and present
Underscoring the change
Highlighting the transformation,
From the regal Draupadi
Through her rebel namesake
Becoming the first citizen of her country

The chief commander of her armed forces
Restoring the glory
Intrinsically connected with an ancient name.

*   Renowned Indian author, Mahasweta Devi's much-acclaimed
     story
*1   President of India, and the country's first tribal one

42

Weaver at the Loom

Shuttles and needles
Spindle and thread
Cotton and silks
Hour after hour
Day after day
Month and years
Till eyes fail;
Quietly at the loom
Telling a story
Sadly, we refuse to hear
But the loom.

Opening heart to the fabric at hand
Bending over the loom
The story of a weaver
Caught in a sari
A drape
Ah! What beautiful motifs
Brilliant hues
And silky fabrics
Blending into one
But, each length carries a unique tale
That often,
Isn't a happy one…

A life of poverty,
Nearly shorn of respect,
That once was a livelihood
Much admired and well-paid.
Today, it rapidly fails to sustain –
This trade from forefathers
Brings neither happiness nor wealth,
Only a life, swathed in needs
In the folds of Muga and Kanchipuram silk.

Machines have taken over
The hand looms
Leaving behind just a handful
Working behind the looms;
Mind you,
Spinning, shuttling and needling is not easy
Takes time, a long time
From cotton to thread to cloth
But in today's racing world
Where patience is pricy
To hear the story
Appreciate the skill
Feel the pain,
Comes not easy.

You pay a cost for this
Nothing comes free
So, is handwoven
Fabulous, rich, expensive
Exclusive is what I fear
It might go on to be...

If the weaver and his art must survive,
This symbol of our freedom
Our struggle,
Our history and culture
Join hands we must,
Spin a way out
For the weaver,
Re-*charkha**...

*   The *Charkha* or the spinning wheel, so interwoven with India's
    freedom struggle, came to symbolize its self-reliance.

43

Little Jagia

My little *Jagia*
Loves her new name
And must it not be so
Besotted with all things Korean
Including a Korean name.
'Honey' or 'Darling' – is all it means
A perfect name
Google searched, herself.

Fun and frolic Jagia loves much
Her soulful laughter rings in my ear
So innocent, full of joy
Yet, mischievous to the core
Pure and carefree
From her cradle days,
Let it always ring so
Forever, and so pure.

Innocent, playful, funny
Jagia juggles,
With words and ideas;
Creative with the brush,
Weaves her imagination
Around tales and riddles,
When all at once,
Pop she questions –

"A vegetable with a cap" –
At a loss for an answer,
She responds, mischievously –
"A *cap*sicum, must it not".

She whirls and swirls on the ballet floor,
Skips and jumps and swings around,
But a ballerina,
She does not aspire to be.
A foodie,
Jagia loves to eat and try,
Bakes cakes and cookies,
Totally out of the blue,
Mixing ingredients
At her whim and fancy
She churns out surprises
Very pleasant too.

Now, she no longer
Whiles away with her Barbies
It is the tab, the mobile,
And all things online
That replaces the sexy doll
Catching her fancy
On the small glittering screen.
She dabbles with fun time reels,
On her channel,
Bringing tears of laughter
With pranks and random jokes
To relief dull moments.

Yet, nothing fancies Jagia more
Than a boyband she adores,

A group of seven
That got her hooked,
Like many young and old
All around the globe.

Yet she blubs much,
From laughter to tears
Is but a moment away,
But, with Jagia's frolicky spirit
She always will be for me –
Lively and chatty
Touching my life,
With love and laughter,
Letters, arty tokens of affection
Kisses, hugs and more.

44

The Beehive

Bees and buzz
Bees and buzz
And the next moment
They are all GONE!

A flurry like mad
Chaos and confusion
Some falls dead
While others try to escape
Some resilient, resolute to protect
The only treasure they know
Their honey
The only home they know,
Their beehive,
THEIR LIFE.

Yet none survives,
In hundreds, they perish
Wither and die,
A torturous death
Cursed last few minutes
Suffocated with toxic gas
Not knowing why this fate
What was their mistake.

Unsuspecting, innocent,
Hard-working, gullible
They know only to slog
Buzz busily, collect nectar
From far and near
For a sweet future…
For that ONE DAY.

But our greed got in the way
We took their home and honey away
And, that one day never came
Bees and buzz, all gone
Scattered and destroyed
All quietened away.

45

*Kashmiri Bhaiya**

A common sight every winter
On chilled foggy mornings,
Sunny afternoons and smogy twilights –
The Kashmiri *wala**
The Kashmiri *bhaiya*,
Sauntering from street to street
On business though
Lugging hefty bundles
Woolen stoles and shawls,
Clothes in silk and
And, of late in cotton too,
Exquisitely designed in bright hues
All in Kashmiri style too.

Come winter, the Kashmiri Bhaiyas
We frequently see on the streets
Walking with backs bent,
Bent with heavy load – they carry
Of piles of clothes, and worries of home
In a riot of colours, silver and gold
Memories of mountains and cries of *chinar**[1]
Blanketed in snow and cold.

They travel hundreds of miles,
To warmer climes
Carrying memories of dreaded Kashmiri winters,

Friends and families,
Left behind in difficult times
No, not a vacation,
It is not their holiday,
They cannot afford one;
They travel across India
To just earn some bread.

These handsome men,
Yes, only men, never a woman,
Come this far, trading their wares
While they leave behind, the women,
To face their own struggles
In the freezing valley, in that inhospitable clime
For women, mustn't they stay back
To worry and care,
Look after, the young and old.

Yes, these handsome men
With sharp noses and sharper features,
Fair of complexion,
Though often, not very tall,
Away, they come from home
Leaving behind everything they love
For money and some food.

Unknowingly the Kashmiri *Bhaiyas*
Become messengers of peace and brotherhood
Delegates of their art and culture,
Quietly but surely
They pass it on,
Enriching their brethren while keeping them warm.

But, come summer, they are gone
Suddenly disappear like mist and dew,
Their weaves no longer in demand,
But packed up and shelved away
For another winter,
Months away.

Wrapped up in Kashmiri comfort
I feel the colours many
Swathed in unique embroidery
Their silk and wool, the touch and feel
But I also feel,
Stronger than the silk, more vibrant than their colours
Their pain, their hardship
Their toil, their labour
Their worry, their solitude
Their travail,
Their travel,
Their brilliant eyes,
Giving away, their loneliness,
Their doubt, and pain.

*   Bhaiya – in Hindi, means brother
*1   Chinar – these trees found throughout Kashmir are an integral
part of their tradition.

46

Believe

Believe, I need to
That beautiful emotion
The crux of human existence
Believe,
That makes us humans
The foundation on which we loose ourselves
We love,
Yes, trust we must, to carry on,
We must believe.

Our heart craves to believe
Have faith, trust and love,
Immerse in sublime emotions!
Add sweet meaning to our meaningless lives,
Ring in joy, hand-in-hand with sadness
Life in partnership with death.
Yes, believe we must
Or, shouldn't we at least try –
For our sake,
To help us stay rooted
But what shall we do
When the head denies
Heart betrays, emotions shattered,
Soul betrayed.

It was only the other day,
That there were gruesome footage
Of a young woman,
Full of love and life,
Hacked to death
To pieces many, by her beloved,
Whom she trusted, had placed her faith.

But, alas, that was just one
Another sister poisoned to death
By her own brother
Whom she believed
For having loved, for having married another
Against his wish.

A boy, a young student all of fifteen
A bright mind, full of promise and life
Snuffed away, by a poisoned drink
By a mother, another boy's mother
For scoring higher
Just a few marks,
Yes, hard to believe!

No, matter how hard,
We keep our believe
For fear,
We lose our humanity
Or else,
How do we LIVE!

47

Winter is Here!

Winter is cold, hard and grey
Who said so?
Methink, I have read it so…
But,
Winter I know
Is full of life and laughter
When gone are the scorching days
The summer heat burning us out,
When in sweat and dust, must we toil
There seems no respite
The heat only increasing, everyday.

Winter harsh, cold and grey
Only in foreign language
Where it had once come from
In a foreign place, in a land far away,
A different clime,
Where winters are, indeed, cold and grey
When all around is freezing,
Covered in inches and feet of snow
Where the frost bites, sunlight sparse
Where even plants prefer to temporarily die.

It is time to rewrite the winters
Look at in a different way,
When oranges ripen and flowers blossom
Roses that wither in heat now in full bloom,
Season of winter veggies and fruits.
It is the time of the year
When the sunlight is sweetest,
In this season of *gur, pitha-payesh*,*
Delicacies, we love to dig in…
A season of festivals
Following in mad succession,
When people celebrate the season
In picnics and fairs,
Yes, this is the winter I know!

The cold and grey winter, unawares
Stares at me, in bleak desperation
I fathom, wish not to understand
I am sure it's beautiful
But that harshness appeals not to me
The other's version, else's story
A foreign interpretation
In a language, that once upon a time
Was foreign,
Today, we have adopted as our own
Made it our near and dear,
Held it so close
That we now forget,
Once upon a time, it was not our own;
So I decide to rewrite, a different winter
Of vibrant colours,

Warm and cozy, sweet and seductive,
Pretty, coveted and loved,
Yes, this are the winters I love...

*   jaggery and jaggery-based regional delicacies, specially made
during Indian winters when jaggery is plentiful.

48

Wings on Colour*

Have you seen birds
Birds of beautiful colours
In hues brilliant and bright
Be it the beak,
The shine in their eyes,
Their feathers lustrous and light
Perched on a tree
Or on an electric wire
Or, when high in the sky
Those are happy colours
Natural colours
One with nature and sky.

Those are wings on colour
The true wings on colour
As it ought to be
But I keep recalling
Alas, of those different wings
Those wings on colour
O God, what I see
I cry… are these the work of humans
Or, of beasts?

These are wings on colour
Of tiny, pretty, plump
Birds and sparrows, I know not which

Cramped and trapped in small cages
With wings clipped, just enough,
So that they cannot fly
But big enough, to get a buy
These are wings of colour
That will never fly.

Wings of colour that will never know the sky
The freedom of what it is to fly
Dyed in strong artificial dyes
Not just those sad clipped wings
But their entire beings
In bright ugly colours
Not just tainting,
Diseasing their small cute plump bodies
In skin rashes and cruelty
A life of torture, of inhumanity
These living images
Shouting out loud
Of our insensitivity.

---

* Somehow, I, have always felt that the title of former President of India, A.P.J. Abdul Kalam's book *Wings on Fire* a catchy one... this however, is a retake of the title, if I may, conveniently tweaked to suit the subject of this poem (which is vastly different from the book). This is not to disrespect President Kalam's book in any way.

49

Loss

Loss or the fear of losing,
Which is the scarier, the worst,
The other more stronger, short-lived,
But loss, is prolonged
Never ending, silent and cold
Burns a hole in you,
Where it dwells forever,
Right in the heart
Till our very end
When we breathe our last.

Loss of a dear one
Once unsurmountable
Hurts less with time
But dwells forever,
Cozily sitting in a corner
Lifting its head from time to time
Awakened by a memory, a place, a thing
Or, even a smell.

In our short lives,
We burn some holes
The biggest and the deepest
For the ones, we love most
Mourning their love, their voice

Their touch as they sat next to us
Their words, their looks,
Their Presence in their absence.

The craving never dies, completely…
Faded but burning still
To hold them in our arms
To feel their touch,
The longing to love and kiss
The deep longing to have them back
Never dies.

One that is gone never comes
We are told with authoritative certainty,
Who doesn't know this…
We don't need affirmations,
Of certainty, that quietly resides
At the back of our minds;
The truth we acknowledge and admit
Yet, too painful to accept,
Hoping for a miracle;
But deep down the longing lurks,
To hold, to love, be loved,
Never ceases,
Just as love never ceases,
Burning a hole in us,
Where loss dwells cozily
And ours forever.

50

Self-Love

'Self-love' – o, those words again…
Bores down on me
With boring regularity
Be it where I look
You cannot escape that word –
'Self-love'…
On the lips of every other person
It has become, the talk of the town
Used, abused, over-used
Jaded it sounds to my ears
The women on my socials
The eye-catching advertisements
The media and the preacher
It has become a cliché
Hackneyed and much-understood
A fashion statement
Worn casually on the sleeves
By the chic and elite
Uttered stylishly, from painted lips
With manicured nails for company
Delicately poised, over a glass of wine.

Now, I can no longer bear
My inside screams
Shut my eyes and ears
Yet unable to blur out the conjoined word.

Curious to know, I question
If others understood
Whereas, I didn't,
Try as much, yet I cannot escape its ring
I google for its meaning.

Books have been written
Entire treatises made
Declarations of self-love pledged,
I fathom not,
Over a concept so old
Why so much waste…
Trying to give it a new make-over
Has not one loved oneself the most
From the beginning of dawn
Self-love or loving oneself
Ought I to distinguish –
Loving oneself has been our prime concern
Always was and will always be
Camouflaged, or straight-forward
It matters not,
Women and men,
With or without
Preaching and propaganda
Will indulge in self-love
Now, and till the end of time.

51

Covid

You came out of nowhere
And took the world by storm
An orphan, with no past
A future, unborn..
The world can only guess
Where you came from
The eastern Orient – beyond the Himalayas
Or, somewhere in the West?
A mystery, destined to remain unsolved
Only your presence felt.

You came, creeping on us
Slow at first, picking up speed
To become THE WHIRLWIND
Gaining momentum
Not sure, if slowing your pace
Figured anywhere in your list;
Taking as many lives, devouring greedily and hungrily
An unappeased hunger, thirst for blood,
Destroying families, homes and lives
Young, old and even the new born.
You spared not, in your wake,
You grew too strong, too powerful
The invincible, the unconquerable

Destroyer,
Of peace, happiness and lives untold.

You became a celebrity overnight
The evil superhero, the invisible!
Your name in the lips of all
Much feared and dreaded,
With unseen ruthlessness
You dolled death free and fast
To many, too many.
The doctors, nurses, paramedics,
Who put up valiantly against you
Buckled, bent and succumbed
In numbers unprecedented
Beating easily the olden wars.

Today you are weak,
Not completed defeated yet,
You refuse to give up
Rearing your cruel self,
Here and there
And, from time to time;
Yet know, that the human spirit
Can be unforgiving too
It will forever remember
Never forgive you.

52

Déjà Vu

I did not search for it
Somehow, I just knew
A creepy, unsettling feeling
It ought to be there –
I have never explored before
But its presence was familiar
Like a second skin
Not mine – hence, a certain degree of difference
But someone else's
Could perhaps, and I am sure
Could belong to many.

These feelings, emotions,
Words spoken and unspoken
Expressed, cried over, laughed at
Belongs to me
And yet I know
Deep down, it belongs, to you…
To too many,
To me and my kind
Women and men
Whom I can hug,
Smile and share
Cry and fail to understand,
Yet, endeavour to empathize.

I am sure
These can be as much their words
Their fears, feelings, insecurities
As surely as they are mine.
Their déjà vu,
Their expressions, uttered through mine.

53

Wielding the Pen

Intertwined Experiences

I try to wield the pen
I pick it up, but it drops
From my hand,
Again, again and again…
I try to understand what it means,
To you and to me;
'Wield the pen'
Is it to write – scribble thoughts,
Longings, dreams and hopes,
Speaking of daring to dream
Weaving dreams into words,
Struggling in and out
Picking up a little bit of courage
Feeble attempts to find the words…

Words, that have remained unuttered
Hanging in the air
Frozen like icicles
Or, buried under dust, grime and decay
Depending on the clime and place
From East to West
The story once untold,
Remained the same

Slowly finding manifestation
Baby steps, one at a time
Fragile attempts to express the expressionless.

Yet nothing remains forever suppressed
The feeble too finally wields the pen
Scribbles down – thoughts,
Weakly at first
And then pours out
One day, unleashing in torrents
All vented, unexpectedly expressed,
Speaking for oneself and others,
Of tears, and pain,
Suffering and fortitude
Of patience and of breaking free,
About joy of a flight
The restrictions and bondage
The difficult steps
Yet, finally Redefining Definitions.

Today, I too
Have learnt from you
All of you before me
Who have struggled and been stifled
But finally wielded the pen.
You, opened the path
Laid the carpet
Made utterance and mutterance easy for me,
To walk down, all smooth sail
Express yours and mine
Of lives woven together
Our joys and sorrow – *INTERTWINED...*

Capable today, to laugh and smile away
At our fears,
For at last, you and I
Have learnt to wield the pen.